The World Came to My Place Today

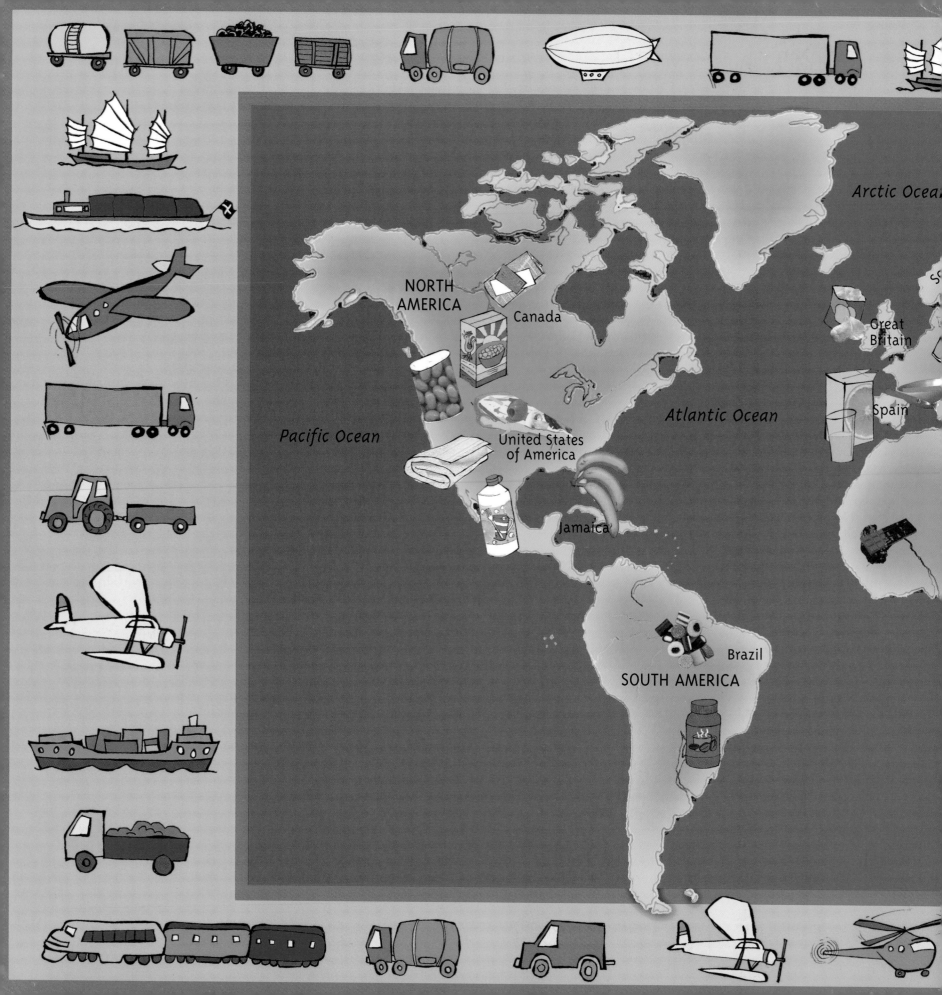

NORTH
AMERICA

Canada

United States
of America

Jamaica

Pacific Ocean

Atlantic Ocean

Arctic Ocean

Great
Britain

Spain

SOUTH AMERICA

Brazil

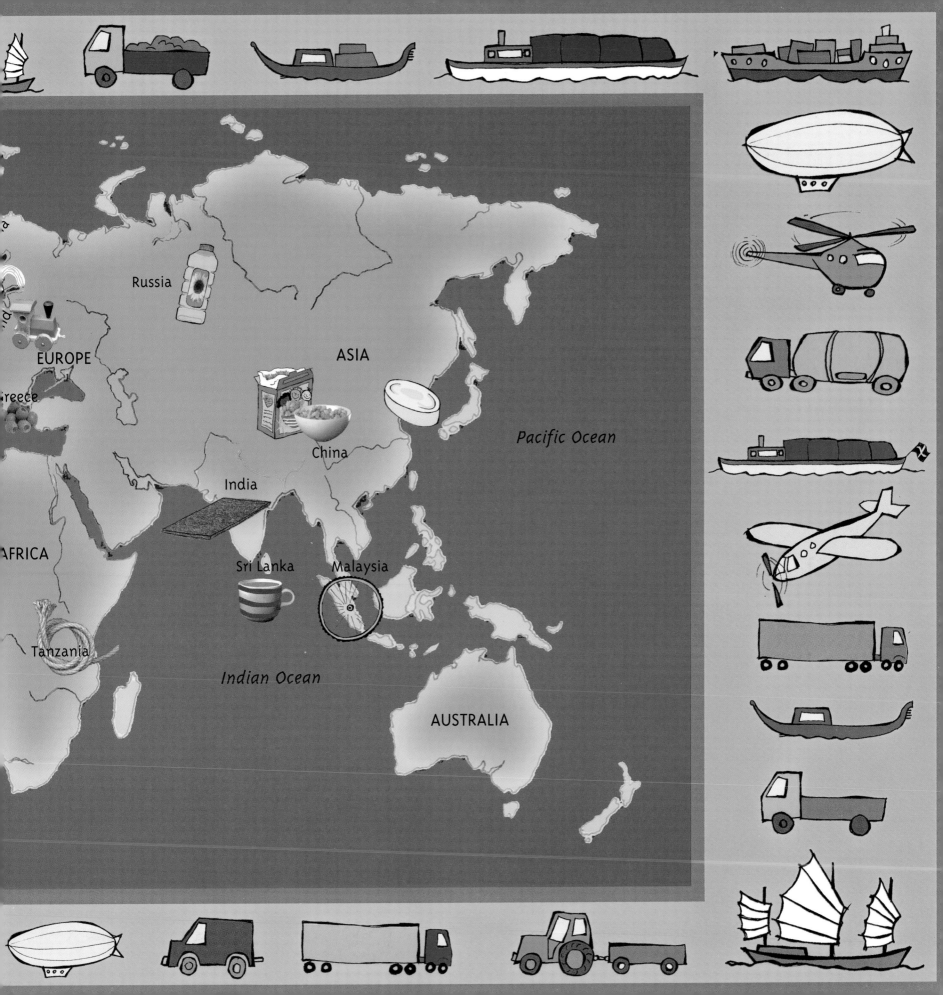

To Jake and Charlie and all other children everywhere.
Enjoy your food, and travel the world with it.
Look after the plants that look after you.
J.R.

For Daisy and Martha
L.H.R.

THE WORLD CAME TO MY PLACE TODAY
AN EDEN PROJECT BOOK 1 90 391902 9

Published in Great Britain by Eden Project Books,
an imprint of Transworld Publishers

This edition published 2004

1 3 5 7 9 10 8 6 4 2

Text copyright © Jo Readman, 2002
Illustrations copyright © Ley Honor Roberts, 2002
With thanks to WHSmith plc for permission to use their globe in this book.
Photographs © Eden Project with thanks to L.H.R., J.R., Ron Readman, Andrew Ormerod,
Phil Gendall and John Bertram

TRANSWORLD PUBLISHERS
61–63 Uxbridge Rd, London W5 5SA
A division of The Random House Group Ltd

RANDOM HOUSE AUSTRALIA (PTY) LTD
20 Alfred Street, Milsons Point, Sydney,
New South Wales 2061, Australia

RANDOM HOUSE NEW ZEALAND LTD
18 Poland Road, Glenfield, Auckland 10, New Zealand

RANDOM HOUSE (PTY) LTD
Endulini, 5A Jubilee Road, Parktown 2193, South Africa

THE RANDOM HOUSE GROUP Limited Reg. No. 954009

www.Kidsatrandomhouse.co.uk
www.edenproject.com

A CIP catalogue record for this book is available from the British Library.

Printed in Singapore

The World Came to My Place Today

Jo Readman

Illustrated by Ley Honor Roberts

Eden Project Books

Flora's got SPOTS all over,
and that means George can't
go out today.
"Never mind," said Grandpa. "Look, I've
brought the world to your place instead."

"I wish the world could really come to visit me, Grandpa," sighed George.
"It already has," said Grandpa. "The rice in your cereal came from China, and the oranges in your juice grew in sunny Spain."

Orange juice is squeezed out of oranges. Oranges grow on trees in warm, sunny places, like Spain and California.

This breakfast cereal is made from puffed-up rice grains.

Rice plants grow in warm, wet places.

"Grrr...woof, woof, woof," barked Buster as the postman delivered the letters.

"Careful, Buster," warned Grandpa.

"This paper was made from trees in Canada.

And even the doormat is made from coconuts in India."

"Really?" said George. "It doesn't look very tasty."

Paper is made of mushed-up wood. Spruce and pine trees, for wood and paper, grow in cool places, like Canada and Scandinavia.

Doormats are made from the hairy coats of coconuts. Coconuts grow on coconut palm trees in hot, wet places, like India.

"Wheee! I'm off round the world on my bike, now," said George. "Why not visit Malaysia," laughed Grandpa, "to find the rubber trees that made your tyres? But it might be quicker to go down the garden and dig up a potato. That's what your crisps are made from."

Rubber is a white liquid that comes from rubber trees when the bark is cut. Rubber trees grow near hot, wet rainforests in south-east Asia.

Crisps are fried thin slices of potato. Potatoes grow in gardens and farms all over the world.

At lunchtime they all had pizza.
"I don't like olives," said George.
"Buster does!" said Grandpa.
"Maybe he knows they've
travelled all the way from
Greece. But the rest of the
pizza is made out of wheat
from America."

Pizza bases, like bread, are baked from flour, which is ground-up grains of wheat.

Wheat is grown on farms in places that are not too hot and have plenty of rain, like Europe and North America.

Olives grow on olive trees. They are soaked in salty water before you eat them.

Olive trees grow in warm, sunny places, like Greece, Italy and Spain.

Ding dong! "Delivery from the supermarket!"
The world really HAD come to
George's place today.

"Are you going to help unpack, George?" said Grandpa.
George started by checking that the chocolate tasted OK.

Bananas grown in Jamaica.

Cornflakes made from maize grown in the United States.

Washing-up liquid scented with lemons from California.

Baked beans made from haricot beans grown in the United States.

Coffee ground from coffee beans grown in Brazil.

Sunflower oil made from sunflower seeds in Russia.

Soap made with oil from oil palms grown in Asia.

"Look what I've made, Grandpa," cried George.
"I'm going to sail the high seas in search of chocolate."
"Can I come too?" asked Grandpa. "We should go to west
Africa first. That's where we'll find the cocoa beans growing."

Chocolate is made from ground-up cocoa beans. The beans are found in the pods of cocoa trees that grow in west Africa.

Poor Grandpa was getting tired. "Swing me higher!" begged Flora. "Lucky this rope is strong," he puffed. "It was made in Africa."

"My train is off to find some more toys," said George.

"It'll have to go to Poland, then," said Grandpa, "where the wood came from."

This rope comes from Tanzania, in Africa.
It is made from the leaf fibres of the sisal plant.

Wooden toys are often carved from the wood of beech trees. Beech trees grow in northern Europe.

"Mum's home!" shouted George. "And she's brought us some sweets!"

"Sugar from Brazil," said Grandpa. "And liquorice from France."
"Now, where can I get a nice cup of tea?" said Mum.
"How about Sri Lanka!" laughed Grandpa.

Sugar is squeezed out of the stems of sugar cane (or the roots of sugar beet). Sugar cane plants grow in tropical countries, like Brazil.

Tea leaves grow on bushes in warm, damp places, such as India, China and Sri Lanka. The green leaves are fermented and dried before they are put into tea bags.

At suppertime Grandpa needed a rest.
"Even though Grandpa's asleep," whispered George, "the world hasn't stopped coming to our place, has it, Mum?"
"Oh, no," said Mum. "Look at the tomatoes in your soup. They come from Italy."

Tomato soup is made
from cooked, mashed-up tomatoes.
Tomato plants grow in warm
places all over the world.

George took his globe into the bathroom.
"Time to brush your teeth now," said Mum.
"Smell the mint in the toothpaste – you can
grow mint in the garden, you know."

But George was busy showing Flora his ship carrying spices across the bubbly Indian Ocean.

Towels are made from cotton.
Cotton plants grow in hot dry places, such as the southern states of America and parts of China and India.

The minty flavour in toothpaste comes from peppermint oil, which is squeezed from the leaves of peppermint. Peppermint grows all over Europe and the United States.

"I liked it when the world came to my place," said George sleepily.
"Will it come again tomorrow?"
Mum kissed him goodnight.
"Of course it will," she said.
"The world comes to your place every day."

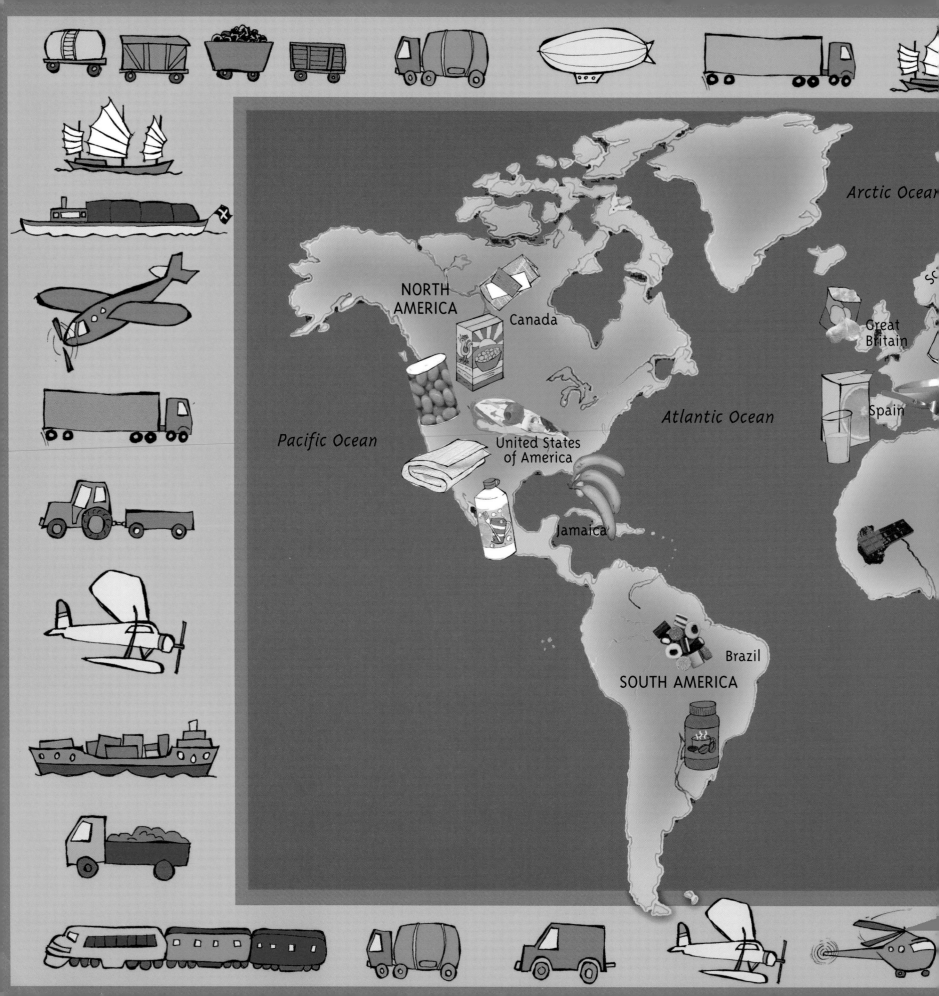

NORTH
AMERICA

Canada

Atlantic Ocean

Pacific Ocean

United States
of America

Jamaica

Arctic Ocean

Great
Britain

Spain

Brazil

SOUTH AMERICA

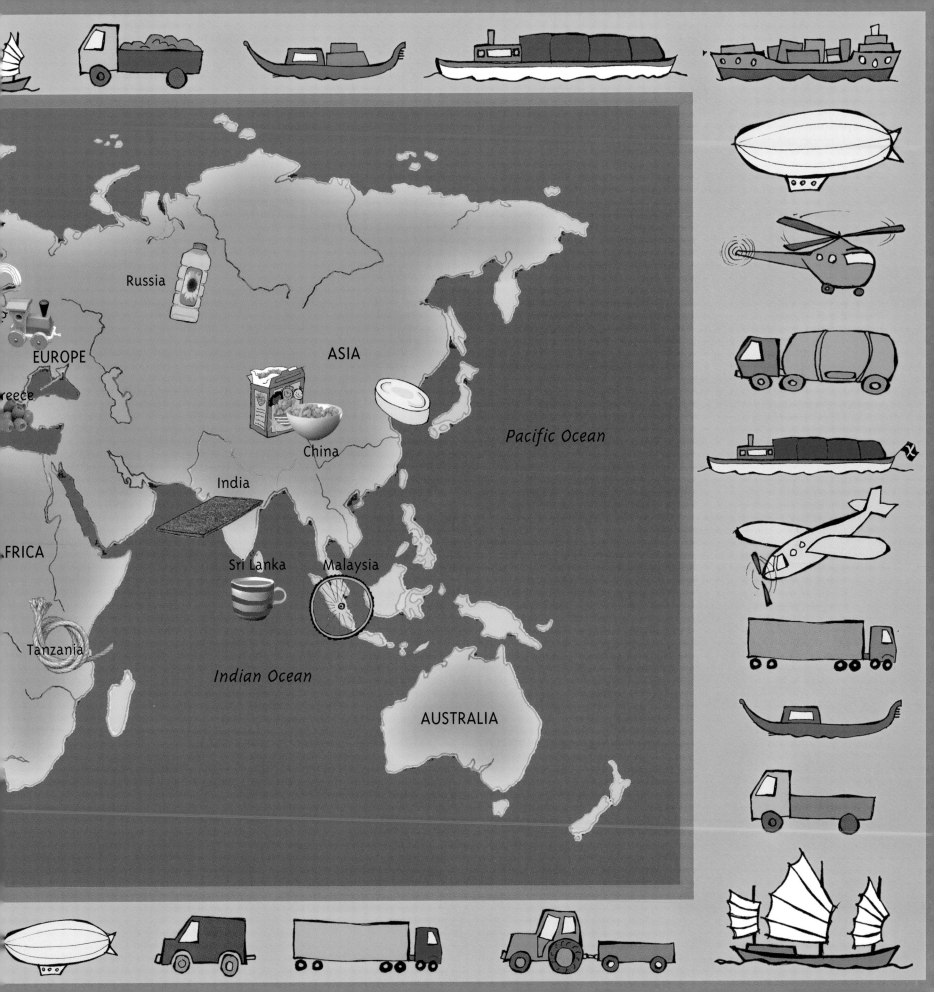

eden project

Deep in a giant crater in Cornwall are the two biggest greenhouses in the world — the famous Biomes of the Eden Project, where you can enter a lush tropical rainforest or the dry, scented lands of the Mediterranean.

They were created to show people just how much we depend on plants to feed and clothe us. You can see for yourself the trees and fruits and flowers that become chocolate, baked beans, rubber tyres, cotton T-shirts, paper for books and many others.

You can discover plants at Eden through music, art and storytelling and through Eden project books too! Take a look at CHARLOTTE VOAKE'S beautiful A CHILD'S GUIDE TO WILD FLOWERS (Eden Project Books, April 2004).